PROGRAMMING FOR PROBLEM SOLVING

BEGINNER'S GUIDE TO LEARN PROGRAMMING IN C

DAVID LIVINGSTON J

Contents

Fundamentals of Computers & Programming

This section introduces some of the fundamental concepts of Computers such as Characteristics of Computers, Generations of Computer, Classification of Computers, Functional Organization of Computers, and Computer Hardware and Software. They are presented in the first five chapters as listed below:

1. Introduction to Computers

2. Generation of Computers

3. Classification of Computers

4. Basic Computer Organization

5. Types of Computer Software

6. Introduction to Programming

7. Structured Programming Approach

8. Planning a Computer Program

CHAPTER ONE

Introduction to Computers

Computer is a calculating device, which receives input from the user, analyses the input by applying a pre-defined set of instructions to produce required output. For instance, in a ticket reservation system, we enter the details of passenger such as name, age, gender and the date of journey as input. The computer will then analyze the given data and make a reservation.

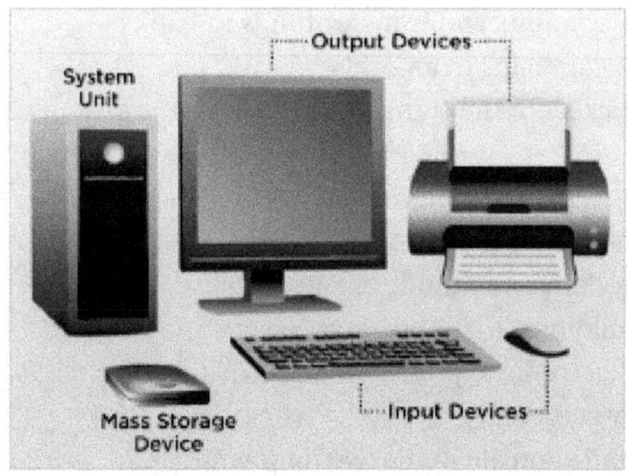

Fig. 1.1 Components of a Modern Digital Computer

A computer is also called a **data processor**, because it can receive, store, process and retrieve any kind of data using its processing unit. For instance, we can use computer to store the details of employees in an organization, which include personal details, pay details, and leave details. The stored information can be retrieved later to analyze the performance of employees and to print pay slips for them.

Computers are everywhere. Every day we come in contact with and use dozens of computers, sometimes without even knowing it. When we stop by the ATM to withdraw cash, a computer performs the calculations, updates our account and dispense the actual cash with the help of mechanical parts controlled by the computer. At supermarket, computers are used to tell us how much our groceries cost. Computers can also provide us with real-time weather reports; driving directions, and in modern vehicles even notify emergency response teams if we're in an accident.

Two important characteristics of a computer are: speed and accuracy. Computers operate at very high speed and execute several million instructions in one second. They also perform their operations with a very high degree of consistent accuracy. Because of these features, computers are used in various fields, where there is a need for doing calculations or data processing speedily, accurately and diligently. Some of the tasks that can be performed using computers are listed below:

- To prepare documents and perform data processing jobs in offices
- To maintain accounts and transfer funds in banks
- To prepare salary slips in an office
- To reserve tickets in the transportation sector, e.g., Railways, Airlines etc.
- To regulate traffic lights on roads
- To control machines in factories
- To control robotics and modern automobiles
- To design buildings, roads etc.
- To control electronic appliances such as Air Conditioners, TVs & VCRs,
- To forecast weather
- To control and simulate defense equipment
- To perform scientific and industrial research.

Characteristics of Computers:

Now-a-days computer is playing a major role in the life of human being. It has been widely used like any other electronic gadgets that include television, telephone or mobile phone. It solves the human problems very quickly as well as accurately. Some of the characteristics of a modern computer are described below:

1. **Speed:** The computer is a very high speed electronic device. The operations on the data inside the computer are performed through electronic circuits according to the given instructions. The data and instructions flow along these circuits with high speed as fast as the speed of light. Computer can perform million of billion of operations on the data in one second. The computer generates signals during the operation process therefore the speed of computer is usually measure in mega hertz (MHz) or gega hertz (GHz). It means million cycles units of frequency is hertz per second. Different computers have different speed.

2. **Arithmetical and Logical Operations:** A computer can perform arithmetical and logical operations. In arithmetic operations, it performs the addition, subtraction, multiplication and division on the numeric data. In logical operation it compares the numerical data as well as alphabetical data.

3. **Accuracy:** In addition to being very fast, computer is also very accurate device. it gives accurate output result provided that the correct input data and set of instructions are given to the computer. It means that output is totally depended on the given instructions and input data. If input data is in-correct then the resulting output will be in-correct. In computer terminology it is known as garbage-in garbage-out.

4. **Reliability:** The electronic components in modern computers have very low failure rate. A modern computer can perform very complicated calculations without any difficulty and produces consistent (reliable) results.

5. **Storage:** A computer has internal storage (memory) as well as external or secondary storage. In secondary storage, a large amount of data and programs (set of instructions) can be stored for future use. The data and programs stored in a secondary storage are available any time for processing.

6. **Retrieving data and programs:** The data and program stored on the storage media can be retrieved very quickly for further processing. It is also very important feature of a computer.

7. **Automation:** A computer can automatically perform operations without interfering the user during the operations. It controls automatically different devices attached with the computer. It executes automatically the program instructions one by one.

8. **Versatility:** Versatile means flexible. Modern computer can perform different kind of tasks one by one of simultaneously. It is the most important feature of computer. At one moment your are playing game on computer, the next moment you are composing and sending emails etc. In colleges and universities computers are use to deliver lectures to the students. The talent of computer is dependent on the software.

9. **Communications:** Today computer is mostly used to exchange messages or data through computer networks all over the world. For example the information can be received or send throug the internet with the help of computer. It is most important feature of the modern information technology.

10. **Diligence:** A computer can continually work for hours without creating any error. It does not get tired while working after hours of work it performs the operations with the same accuracy as well as speed as the first one.

11. **No Feelings:** Computer is an electronic machine. It has no feelings. It detects objects on the basis of instructions given to it. Based on our feelings - taste, knowledge and experience, we can make certain decisions and judgments in our daily life. On the other hand, computer cannot make such judgments on its own. Its judgments are totally based on instructions given to them.

12. **Consistency:** People often have difficulty to repeat their instructions again and again. For example, a lecturer feels difficulty to repeat a same lecture in a class room again and again. Computer can repeat actions consistently (again and again) without loosing its concentration:

     ◦ To run a spell checker (built into a word processor) for checking spellings in a document.
     ◦ To play multimedia animations for training purposes.
     ◦ To deliver a lecture through computer in a class room etc.

13. **Precision:** Computers are not only fast and consistent but they also perform operations very accurately and precisely. For example, in manual calculations and rounding fractional values (That is value with decimal point can change the actual result). In computer however, you can keep the accuracy and precision upto the level, you desire. The length calculations remain always accurate.

CHAPTER TWO

Generations of Computers

The early computers, which used vacuum tubes to control the flow of electronic signals, are called **First Generation Computers**. The computers of this generation are: ENIAC, EDSAC, EDVAC and UNIVAC. These computers used thousands of Vacuum tubes to do the entire operation.

Fig. 2.1 Generations of Computers

Vacuum Tube is an electronic device that used filaments for producing electronic signals. Its size is about the size of an electric bulb. It produced lot of heat and burn out frequently. Because of the use of Vacuum tubes, first generation computers were too bulky and failed to work too often.

First Generation Computers:

The **ENIAC (1943-1946)**, called Electronic Numerical Integrator And Calculator was the first electronic computer. It was completely developed in 1946 by a team led by Eckert and Mauchly at the University of Pennsylvania in U.S.A.

ENIAC used high-speed vacuum tube switching devices for the control of electronic signals. There were about 19,000 vacuum tubes in ENIAC. It had a very small memory and used wired plug boards as input devices. ENIAC took about 200 μs to add two digits and 2800 μs to multiply. It was primarily designed to calculate the trajectories of missiles.

The computers EDSAC and EDVAC, which were developed after the ENIAC, were called as 'Stored Program' computers, because they were designed to store instructions and data internally after the proposal of Von Neumann in the year 1946. His idea was to store machine instructions in the memory of the computer along with data.

EDSAC (1947-1949), abbreviation for Electronic Delay Storage Automatic Computer, was the first stored program computer. It was developed by a team of Scientists led by Prof. Maurice Wilkes at Cambridge University, U.K. This machine used mercury delay lines for storage.

EDVAC (1946-1952) is the abbreviation for Electronic Discrete Variable Automatic Computer (EDVAC) was the first effort made on the concept of Van Neumann. It used binary form (i.e., 0 and 1: called discrete or digital signals) to store data and instructions of the decimal number system used by human beings.

Computers, which operate on discrete or digital signals like 0 and 1, high or low are called **Digital Computers**, whereas **Analog computers** operate on analog signals, which are continuously varying in nature. Some of the examples for Analog device are Voltmeter, Ammeter and Speedo meter. EDVAC is an example for Digital computer, which used binary values 0 and 1 for storage and calculation.

Universal Automatic Computer (UNIVAC) was the first computer produced for commercial purpose. It was developed in 1951. It was available for commercial use from 1954.

Second Generation Computers:

Bardeen, Brattain and Shockley invented transistor in 1947. Transistors are made of Germanium Semiconductor material. Compared to vacuum tubes, transistors were highly reliable, occupied less space and used only one tenth of the power required by tubes.

The computers, which were made of transistors, are called Second Generation computers. They were introduced around 1959 and lasted till 1965. The use of transistors made 'second' generation computers faster, smaller and reliable.

Magnetic Core Memories were also invented during second-generation of computers. Magnetic core memories were made up of magnetic cores, which are tiny rings (0.02 inch diameter) made of ferrite. They are magnetized in either clockwise or anticlockwise direction to represent 0 and 1. This type of memory was used to construct RAM up to the size of 100 KB.

Other Developments during First Generation:

1. Magnetic disk storage was developed during this period.
2. Higher level languages - FORTRAN, COBOL, ALGOL and SNOBAL were introduced.
3. The early operating system called Batch Operating System was developed during this time. For e.g., the Batch OS used in IBM 7000 series computer.
4. Commercial applications like Payroll, Inventory Control, Marketing, Production Planning and General Ledger were rapidly developed.

Third Generation Computers:

Integrated Circuits (ICs) were used as the switching device in third generation computers. Germanium transistors were replaced with Silicon transistors in the construction of CPU. Because of the use of Silicon transistors in ICs, the switching speed and reliability of CPU increased by a factor of 10. Power dissipation and the size of CPU were decreased by a factor of 10. This resulted in increase in speed of the third generation computers was 1 MIPS. The System/360 introduced by IBM around 1965 was the first third generation computer.

An IC is a small chip consists of electronic components like transistors, resistors and capacitors on a silicon metal plate. The components were integrated together on a silicon material in order to eliminate the wired interconnection between components.

The technologies used for the construction of ICs of third generation were SSI and MSI. SSI technology can integrate about 10 transistors in a chip. The integration capacity was increased 10 times in MSI technology to hold up to 100 transistors in one chip.

Other Developments during Second Generation:

1. Time-sharing OS like multiprocessing, multiprogramming and multi-user OS were introduced to increase programmer productivity.
2. The High-level language PL/1 of IBM was emerged. Many important on-line systems like dynamic Production control system, Airline reservation system, and Interactive query system were implemented.
3. Significant improvements were made in the design of Core memories. As a result, the size of the main memory reached about 4 MB. Magnetic disk memory was also available up to the size of 100 MB.
4. The standard I O devices keyboard and monitor were newly introduced.

Fourth Generation Computers:

Fourth generation computers used LSI and VLSI technologies for the construction of CPU, memory and supporting chips. The VLSI chip used as the switching device in fourth generation computers is called Microprocessor (μP). Introduction of microprocessor as CPU in the fourth generation computer led to the following developments:

1. Extremely powerful Personal Computers (PC) were emerged.
2. Computer cost came down rapidly.
3. Computer's workload was decentralized. As opposed to a Mainframe computer, which uses a single powerful CPU to be shared by many terminals for many applications, a PC has its own μP to do its processing

and can be connected in a network.

LSI & VLSI Technologies:

In LSI Technology, thousands of components were fit onto one chip, whereas in VLSI technologies, 10 to 50 thousands of transistors were integrated onto a single chip. The ability to fit so much onto an area about half the size of one-rupee coin helped diminish the size and price of computers. The other developments that took place during fourth generation are as follows:

1. Magnetic Core memories were replaced by Semiconductor memories for the construction of RAM. Thus RAM with the size of 16 MB and a cycle time of 200 ns were in common use.
2. Hard disk size for the secondary storage was greatly improved in the order of Giga Bytes. 1 GB of disk on PCs became common in 1994.
3. Optical disks like CD-ROM and DVD-ROM (Digital Versatile Disk ROM) emerged as mass storage devices particularly for read only files. The size of the disk was of the order of 600 MB on a 5.25" disk.
4. High-level languages such as C, C++, ADA and PROLOG were developed. CASE tools were also developed for the Analysis and Design of software.
5. Interactive graphic devices and language interfaces to graphic systems were introduced.

Fifth Generation Computers:

The fifth-generation computers are under development. Fifth generation computers will make use of ULSI chips which consist of millions of components into a single IC. Such computers will use intelligent programming, knowledge-based problem solving techniques, high performance multiprocessor system and improved human-machine interfaces.

The input and output for these computers will be in the form of speech and graphic images. Vision system will be incorporated in order to perceive the surroundings. The computers of this age will be able to understand natural languages like English, Japanese, and Hindi. This will diminish the need for learning computer programming languages by programmers.

Using intelligent programming, the user can tell the computer what to do but not how to do. The computer will do the task of programming itself. The first four generations of computers used Von Neumann's architecture for the design of digital computers. In Von Neumann architecture, a processor executes simple instructions in a sequence. But the fifth generation computers will use a different design and architecture.

Data flow architecture will be used as the basic design for the construction of fifth generation computers. There will be an extensive use of parallel processing and PROLOG is going to be the language for performing parallel processing. Special coprocessors will be used to make logical inferences and manage massive amounts of stored knowledge. In General, fifth generation computers will be knowledge-based computers.

CHAPTER THREE

Classification of Computers

Based on the technology used for the construction of CPU in the computers, they are classified as Microcomputers, Mini computers, Mainframe computers and Super computers. Based on the interconnection of computers, we can classify them as distributed computers and parallel computers.

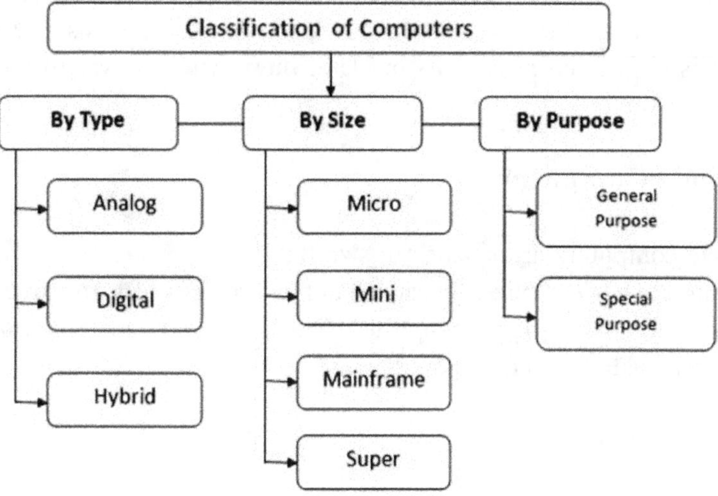

Fig. 3.1 Major Classification of Computers

The computers, which use Microprocessors as their CPU, are called Microcomputers. Today most of the computers are of this category. Based on the mode of use, microcomputers are further classified into Personal computers, Portable computers and Workstations.

Personal Computers (PCs)

Personal computers are computers used by individuals for the purpose of running the stand-alone applications like Word Processing, Spread Sheet etc. Data and applications stored in a PC are not available for sharing by other computer users. To make use of the resources available in a PC from other PCs, it must be connected to a network.

There are two major manufactures of PCs – IBM and APPLE. The machines made by IBM are called IBM PCs. The PCs made by APPLE are called Apple Macintosh. Other manufacturers of PCs also followed the same specifications and design of IBM PCs for the manufacturing of their PCs. The PCs made by third party vendors are known as IBM compatible PCs.

Early PCs designed by IBM had Intel 8088 microprocessors as their CPU. The Operating Systems used by IBM PCs include MS DOS, MS Windows, Windows-NT, UNIX and OS/2. OS/2 is an OS designed specially for IBM PCs.

Apple Macintosh PCs use Apple's proprietary OS, which was well known for its user friendliness. Apple Macintosh machines started using Motorola 68030 as their microprocessors but later they switched over to Power PC 603 processors.

Portable Computers

Portable computers are smaller in size but more powerful than personal computers. They can be easily carried out by professionals, researchers and entrepreneurs while they are on the road. There are two types of portable computers: Palmtop and Laptop PCs.

Palmtop PCs:

Palmtop computers can be held in a palm like a mobile phone kit. Palmtop PCs have a small screen display for both input and output. They can accept handwritten inputs given using electronic pen. A Palmtop PC can also be used as a mobile phone, Fax and email machine. Windows-CE is the OS provided by Microsoft for the operation of Palmtop PCs.

Laptop PCs:

Laptop computers are also known as Notebook computers, which can be kept on the lap for working with it. A Laptop PC weighs around 2 Kg and can be carried out easily while traveling. Laptop PCs cost more - at least 3 to 4 times the cost of desktop PCs of the same capacity because of the use of miniature components, which consume low power. They can run on batteries as they have been designed to conserve energy. The configuration of a Laptop PC includes a keyboard, flat screen liquid crystal display, and a Pentium or Power PC processor.

Workstation PC

Workstations are more powerful and more expensive than desktop computers. They can operate at higher speeds – about 10 times faster than PCs. They are generally used by scientists, engineers, and other professionals for handling huge volume of data. They are more suitable for numeric and intensive graphic applications.

The configuration of a typical Workstation includes: a color Video Display Unit (19 inch monitors), 256 MB to 1 GB RAM as main memory and a hard disk of 40-80 GB. Workstations normally use RISC processors such as SUN's ULTRASPARC, HP's PA 8500 etc. The OS used by Workstations are UNIX, Linux, SUN Solaris and OS-8.

A system called X Windows is used for Workstations to display the status of multiple processes going on during execution. Most workstations have built-in hardware to connect them to a Local Area Network (LAN).

Mini Computers

Minicomputers, also known as mid range computers were first developed as special-purpose mainframe computers. They were introduced for controlling the machines used in manufacturing industry. However, now they are widely used as general-purpose computers. The most popular minicomputer system is VAM, made by Digital Equipment Corporation (DEC).

Mini computers work well for Distributed Computing Environment (DCE), where the processing power is decentralized and distributed across different computers. An example for distributed computer architecture is

Client/Server architecture, in which end users can work with their own microcomputers, and at the same time they can also access and share the resources on the server, which usually is a minicomputer.

Mainframe & Super Computers

Mainframe computers are more powerful than workstations. They are much bigger, faster and more expensive than workstations. Mainframes can process several million-program instructions per second. Organizations like insurance companies, banks, airlines and railways make use of Mainframe computers for handling large number of on-line transactions.

Mainframes can store several Tera bytes of data and transfer data from disk to main memory at several hundred Megabytes/sec. They normally use proprietary operating systems, which usually provide extensive services such as user accounting, file security and control. There are very few manufacturers of mainframe computers, which include IBM and Hitachi.

Supercomputers are the fastest computers available at any given time. They are normally used to solve problems, which require intensive numerical computations. Examples of such problems are: numerical weather prediction, designing supersonic aircrafts, design of drugs and modeling complex molecules. In order to solve such complex problems, many RISC processors are used in the construction of super computers.

The speed of operation of supercomputers is in terms of nanoseconds and even in Pico seconds. Besides arithmetic speed, supercomputers have a large main memory of around 16 GB and a secondary memory of 1000 GB. The speed of data transfer between the secondary memory and the main memory is at least one tenth of the speed of data transfer between main memory and CPU. Such great speed is achieved in super computers through a mechanism called **Parallelism**.

CHAPTER FOUR

Basic Computer Organization

We might be using computers for various applications. Generally, computers perform five basic operations namely: input, storage, processing, output and control.

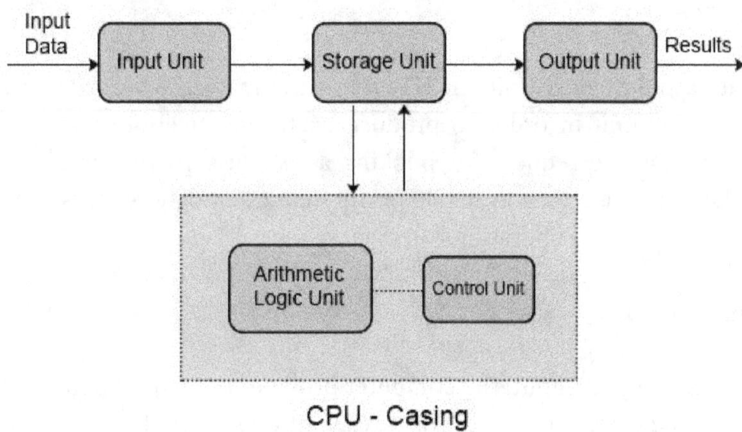

Fig. 4.1 Functional Organizaton of a Digital Computer

A typical computer performs the operations such as:

1. Get the input from the user
2. Store it permanently in a memory device and
3. Process the data to produce information as output.

It also controls the activities performed by its various units.

Input:

Computers receive data from its users. Users feed data (e.g., reservation details) in to a computer through devices such as keyboard and mouse, called input devices. The given data are then processed by applying a set of instructions, called program. Programs instruct a computer what to do with the data.

Storage:

The data/program, which are given as input to the computer are then stored in a hard disk. The Processing Unit (CPU) can get the data/instructions from the storage unit whenever required.

Process:

Arithmetic and Logical Unit (ALU) processes (analyzes) the data available in the storage unit in order to produce useful information. For instance, it may process the request for booking a seat in a particular train on a particular date if a seat is available on the requested date. ALU is the main unit, which performs operations on data.

Output:

After processing the input, the computer provides the required information (result) to the user. For instance, in a reservation system the output may be a printed ticket or display of some information like no. of seats available on a particular date. Commonly used output devices are monitor, printer and plotter.

Control:

All computers have a control unit that controls the manner and sequence of operations. The control unit and the ALU form the Central Processing Unit (CPU) of a system.

The various building blocks of a computer are explained below:

Input Unit:

Input Unit consists of one or more devices, which are used for inputting data and instructions into a computer. Keyboard is the commonly used input device. Other input devices are mouse, scanner, light pen etc. Regardless of the type of input device, all input devices perform the following functions:

1. Accept input from the outside world.
2. Convert the input to a form that computer can understand.
3. Supply the converted data to the computer system for further processing.

Storage Unit:

The storage unit consists of a set of storage devices that store data permanently for later use. For instance, one may like to save a business letter for later reference. The storage devices used in a computer system are classified into two categories – primary storage and secondary storage.

The primary storage (also called the primary memory or main memory) stores and retrieves information very fast. This storage device is generally used to hold programs and data, which are being processed by the CPU. It also holds the data being received from the input unit and the intermediate and final results of the program being executed. This memory is volatile in nature, and hence it looses its contents when the power goes off.

The secondary memory is used like an archive that can hold data and instructions permanently. The program to be executed by CPU is first transferred from the secondary memory to the primary memory before its execution. Similarly, after execution, the resultant data are transferred back to the secondary memory for later use. The secondary memory is slower and cheaper than the primary memory. Examples for secondary memory devices are: Floppy diskette, zip diskette, hard disk and magnetic tape.

Output Unit:

Computers store data and instructions internally in binary form. The input given by the user is converted into binary form in order to perform any processing on it. After processing, the binary data must be converted back to the form understood by the users. This task of converting and delivering the required output in human readable form is done with the help of an output device. Printer and Video Display Unit (VDU; also called Display Screen) are commonly used output devices.

Arithmetic-Logic Unit (ALU):

All calculations are performed in the Arithmetic-Logic Unit (ALU) of the computer. The ALU performs basic operations such as addition, subtraction, multiplication and division. It also performs logical operations such as comparing one number against another and checking if 'A' is less than, equal to or greater than 'B'.

In order to perform a computation by ALU, the control unit first transfers the required data from the storage unit to ALU and allows ALU to perform the required computation. After performing the computation (arithmetic or logical operation), the result is transferred from ALU to the storage unit.

Control Unit:

The control unit controls all other units of a computer. For instance, the input unit does not know where to send the data after it receives input from the user. The control unit gives necessary instructions to the input unit to send the input to the storage unit or to the VDU. In the same way, it controls the flow of data and instructions between the ALU and the storage unit. The control unit also controls what should be sent to the output device and when.

CHAPTER FIVE

Types of Computer Software

The physical devices used to form a computer are called Computer Hardware. Examples for computer hardware are: Monitor, Keyboard, Printer, Hard Disk Drive, and Floppy Disk Drive etc. Computer hardware is responsible for implementing all necessary operations such as accepting user input, storing data, performing calculations, and displaying or printing results.

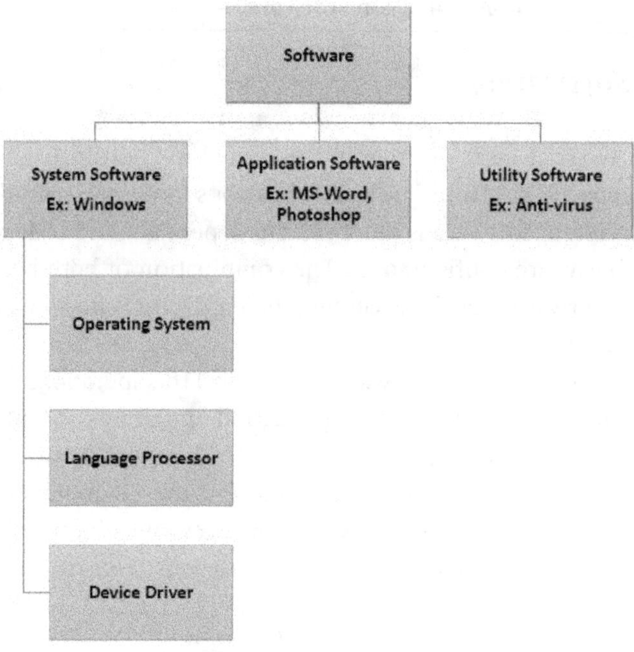

Fig. 5.1 Major Classification of Software

Hardware can't operate on its own. To make them work, we need a set of programs called Software. Software that runs on PCs can be classified into four major categories:

1. Operating Systems like DOS, Windows 95 and UNIX
2. Programming languages such as Basic, Fortran, COBOL, and C++
3. Application programs/packages such as Word Processors, Spreadsheet, and Database Management Systems
4. Other application programs that can do a specific job such as Accounting, Payroll, Billing, Weather forecasting and Ticket Reservation software

Software consists of computer programs that control the operations of computer hardware. Computer programs are nothing but sequence of instructions given by a programmer to perform certain operations on the computer. One of the most critical functions of software is to direct the workings of computer hardware. There are two basic types of software: **System software** and **Application software**.

System Software:

System software is a set of programs designed to coordinate the activities and functions of hardware as well as various programs running on the hardware. System software is more system dependant and is designed for a particular hardware configuration. The combination of both hardware and the system software used for accessing the hardware is known as computer system Platform.

The main use of system software is to control the operations of computer hardware and to support the application programs problem-solving capabilities. An Operating System is one of the system software, which acts as an interface or layer between the user and the computer hardware. It also acts as a Resource Allocator, which manages and allocates resources to specific programs and users for performing various tasks on the computer.

Operating System

An OS consists of control routines for operating a computer and provides an environment for the execution of programs. It may be viewed as an organized collection of Software extension to hardware. The following are the two major goals of an OS:

1. To provide users convenience in operating the system.
2. To make use of the computer hardware efficiently.

The services provided by an OS can be accessed either directly or indirectly through an application program. Users may interact with the OS directly by means of its commands. Application programs have to use the Operating System API calls to access the computer resources like files and I/O devices.

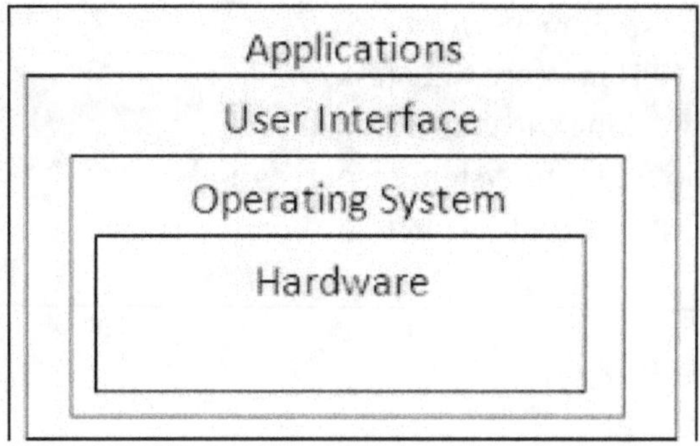

Fig. 5.2 Different Layers of a Computer System

The primary objective of an OS is to increase the productivity of computer hardware. OS may process its workload serially or concurrently. That is, resources in a computer system may be dedicated to a single program until its completion, or they may be allocated dynamically (whenever required) to execute multiple programs simultaneously.

Potential benefits of concurrent execution of multiple programs include increased performance, resource utilization and responsiveness of a computer system. In a multiprogramming OS, multiple active programs share the system resources like processor, memory and I/O devices.

Operating System Functionalities

An OS is a set of computer programs that controls the computer hardware and acts as an interface between the application software and the hardware.

Every OS is usually stored on disk (primary or secondary) and in files. For instance, DOS bundles its functions in a set of files, such as Command.com, Edit.exe, and Copy.exe.

In Windows, the major functionalities are provided in three Dynamic Link Library (DLL) files: GDI32.DLL, KERNAL32.DLL and USER32.DLL. As soon as a computer system is started, portions of the OS are transferred to memory as they are needed. The various functionalities provided by an OS are listed below:

1. Performing common computer hardware functions
2. Providing a User Interface (UI)
3. Providing a degree of hardware independence
4. Managing the system memory
5. Managing the CPU in processing tasks
6. Providing networking capabilities
7. Controlling the access to system resources and
8. Manage the files stored on the hard disk.

The Process & Kernel:

A process or task is an instance of a program in execution. It is the smallest unit of work individually scheduled by an OS. A program is a passive entity, whereas a process is an active entity, with a PC (Program Counter) specifying the next instruction to execute and a set of associated resources. Each multiprogramming OS keeps track of all processes and allocates system resources to them according to policies devised to meet design performance objectives.

Kernel is the core or central part of the operating system that controls the most critical processes. It ties all the components of the OS together and regulates other programs.

Common Hardware Functions:

All application programs perform certain tasks as listed below:

- Get input from keyboard or other input devices
- Retrieve data from disks

- Store data on disks
- Display information on a monitor or printer

Each of these basic functions requires a more detailed set of instructions to complete the particular task. All such functionalities are provided as functions, which contain the set of detailed instructions required by the hardware. A typical OS performs hundreds of such functions, each of which is translated into one or more instructions for the hardware.

User Interface (UI):

A UI allows individuals to access and command the computer system. There are two types of UI: Command-based UI and Graphical User Interface. The early User Interface used in Mainframe and Personal Computer systems was command based.

Command-based OS requires that text commands be given to the computer to perform basic activities. Commands like RENAME and COPY are examples for DOS commands used for renaming and copying the files respectively. On the other hand, GUI based OS provides graphical elements like buttons, frames, pictures and icons to have an interaction with the user.

Hardware Independence:

Hardware independence is achieved through the use of API (Application Program Interface). An API is a set of function definitions, which can be used from an application software to avail the services provided by OS.

Programmers can use APIs to create application software without having to understand the inner workings of the OS. Application software makes use of the services available in the OS by making request through the API. The following figure depicts how API links the application software to the OS:

Hardware Independence

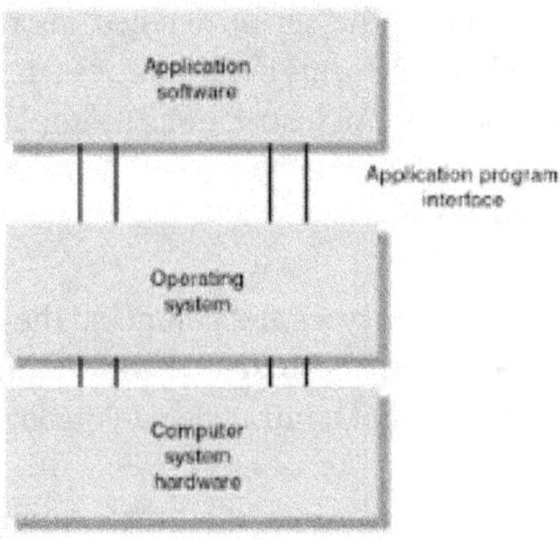

Fig. 5.3 Hardware Indepenance of Software through OS

CHAPTER SIX

Introduction to Programming Languages

Programming languages are coding schemes using which instructions can be given to a computer system for automating some of the tasks performed manually in our day to day life. Using computer languages such as C/C++, professionals develop software of different kinds which include Operating Systems and Application Software.

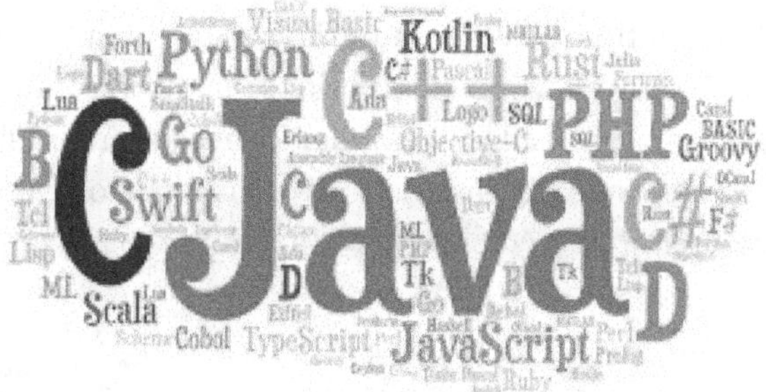

Fig. 6.1 Various Programming Languages of Computer

Software developed using a programming language can help solve a particular problem using computer. Programming languages provide a programmer with a set of keywords, symbols and a system of rules for constructing statements that can be executed by a computer.

The symbols and keywords are having special meaning in the language. The set of rules (called syntax) dictate how the symbols should be combined into statements capable of conveying meaningful instructions to the CPU.

Generations of Programming Languages

The **First Generation** programming language is machine language, which makes use of binary symbols (0s and 1s) for coding. As machine language is the language of the CPU, programs written using machine language can be understood and executed directly by the CPU.

Second Generation Language (2GL) overcomes some of the difficulties faced by programmers of machine language by replacing the binary digits with symbols. Thus, the programs written using second generation language are in more readable form than that of the machine language. Second generation language is also called as Assembly language, since assembly language programs are converted into binary language coding before their execution with the help of a language translator named Assembler.

Third Generation Languages (3GL) are high level languages that use English-like statements and commands. Some of the third generation languages are: BASIC, COBOL, FORTRAN, C, C++ and Java. 3GL languages are easier to learn and use than machine and assembly languages because they use commands that resemble everyday human communication.

With third-generation programming languages, each statement in the language translates into several instructions in the machine language. A special software program called Compiler converts programmer's source code into machine language instructions consisting of binary digits, as shown in below figure:

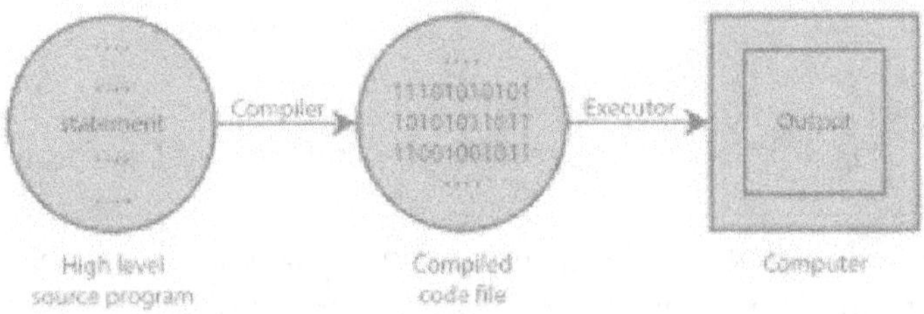

Fig. 6.2 The Role of a Compiler

Fourth Generation Languages (4GL) are languages that support Client/Server technology. 4GL languages have the following characteristics which distinguish them from the third generation languages:

1. Provide features for storing and accessing information from a database.
2. Emphasize what output results are desired rather than how programming statements are to be written.
3. Provide the tools for designing the User Interface screens easily.

4GL languages are of two types: Front-ends and Back-ends. Front-ends are tools that include visual development tools like PowerBuilder, Delphi, Essbase, Focus, Powerhouse and SAS. Back-ends are Database Management Systems (DBMS) such as MS Access, SQL Server, and Oracle. From the front-end, we can access the back-end using a database language called SQL (Structured Query Language) by performing database queries and manipulations.

Fifth Generation Languages (5GL) are Visual Programming languages such as Visual Basic, Visual C++ and PC COBOL. They provide an environment called Integrated Development Environment (IDE), which includes all the necessary tools for program development and deployment. Some of the tools available in an IDE are: Editor, Screen Designer, Code Generator, Compiler and a Debugger.

Moreover, fifth generation languages use a visual or graphical development interface to design the User Interface (UI) and to generate the corresponding source code that can be usually compiled with a 3GL or 4GL language compiler. Microsoft Visual Studio 7, now known as Visual Studio.Net is an example of 5GL that allows programming languages such as COBOL, C++, Perl, SmallTalk, C#, Jscript, Visual Basic, Visual Foxpro and Java to share a single GUI.

Structured Programming and Object-Oriented Programming

Third generation language such as C is also known as Procedural or Structured Programming language, because it separates data elements from the procedure (or action) that will perform certain operation on data. They give more importance to actions (also called procedures) than the data handled by them. In this approach, application programs are divided into smaller programs known as functions. Most of the functions share the data globally.

On the other hand, languages like C++ and Java tie both data and functions (actions) into a single unit called an Object. An object consists of data and functions that operate on the data. Programming languages that are based on the object oriented concepts such as objects, encapsulation, data hiding, polymorphism and inheritance are called Object Oriented languages.

In Object Oriented Programming, any real world entity can be modeled as an object. The whole software is considered as a group of objects that work together to accomplish a particular task. During execution, objects interact with each other by sending messages and receiving responses. For instance, in a program that performs withdrawal from an account, a customer object may send a withdraw message to a bank account object in order to perform withdrawal.

Thus, OOP is defined as a method of programming in which programs are organized as co-operative collections of objects, each of which represents a real world entity. Any object that communicates with another object need not be aware of its internal workings but only its function signatures.

CHAPTER SEVEN

Structured Programming Approach

Software development is a process of creating new software or modifying existing software for meeting the current requirements of its users. This process consists of various stages or phases in it.

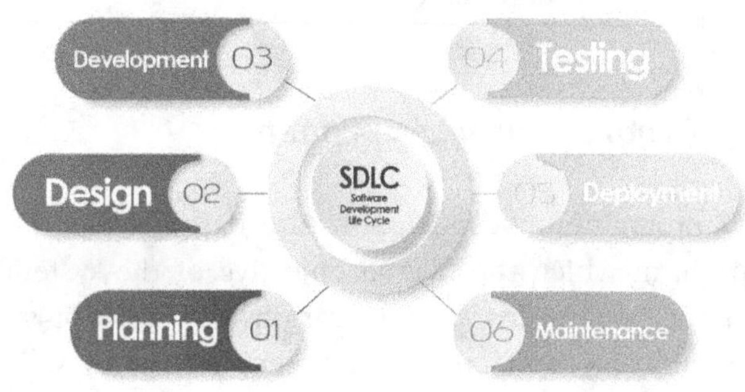

Fig. 7.1 Steps involved in Developing a Software

Steps involved in Software Development process include the following:

1. Problem Definition (Analysis)
2. Program Design
3. Coding / Implementation
4. Testing
5. Deployment

6. Maintenance

A complete set of all these activities involved in developing software is known as Software Development Life Cycle (SDLC). This is because the same sequence of steps are to be followed whenever we develop new software from scratch or modifying existing software for up gradation.

Some small programs like creating a text editor (e.g., Notepad) can be done directly without following all the steps involved in SDLC. But, developing large programs like MS Word or MS Excel involve complexity in areas like understanding the problem domain, meeting the customer needs and delivering a good quality product in time.

To overcome the complexities involved in software development, many methodologies, tools and languages were introduced. Following are two major methodologies introduced for simplifying software development process:

- Structured (Procedural) Programming
- Object Oriented Programming (OOP)

Structured Programming Approach

In structured programming model, software designers tend to use Top-Down approach, in which the overall objective of the system is defined first. Then the system is divided into various sub tasks or sub modules. With this methodology, software development is done by writing a set of sub programs, called functions that can be integrated together to form a complex system.

In Structured programming, the primary focus is on functions. A function is a sub program that performs a specific task using the values given to it through input variables (called parameters) and then returns the result to its caller (main program). Each function consists of a set of program statements and some local variables. A function when invoked behaves as though its code is inserted at the point of its call. The communication between the caller (calling function) and the callee (called function) takes place through parameters. A typical program structure for structured approach is shown below:

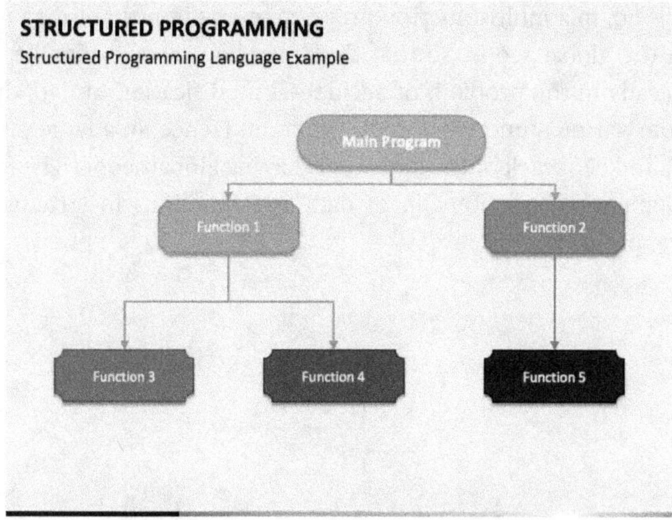

Fig. 7.2 Structured Programming Model

At the time of function call, the control is transferred from the caller to the first statement of the callee (the function itself). All the statements in the function body are executed and then the control is transferred back to the caller to resume the execution of other statements.

Some characteristics exhibited by Structured (also called Procedural-oriented) programming are:

1. Emphasis is on doing things (algorithms)
2. Large programs are divided into smaller programs called functions.
3. Most of the functions share global data.
4. Data move openly around the system from function to function and
5. Employs Top-down approach in program design

Limitations of Structured Programming:

Structured programming was a powerful tool that enables programmers to write moderately complex programs fairly easily. However, as the programs grew larger, this approach failed to show the desired results in terms of bug-free, easy-to-maintain and reusability of programs.

In this approach, very little attention is given to data used by the function. And, in a multi-function program, many important data items are placed in the global scope, so that they may be accessed by all functions. But, this leads to the problem of accidental modification of data due to its access from various functions of the program. Hence, in a large program it is difficult to keep track of the data items having global scope. The following picture depicts the relationship of data and functions in structured (or) procedural programming.

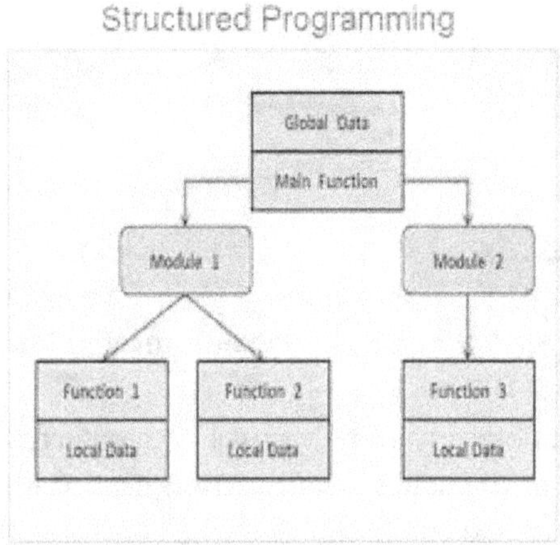

Fig. 7.3 Management of Data and Functions in Structured Programming

Another serious drawback with the procedural approach is that it does not model the real world entities to the elements in a program in a one-to-one manner. This is because the functions are action-oriented and they do not really correspond to the elements of the problem.

Object Oriented Programming - Defined:

Object Oriented Programming is centered on new concepts such as objects, classes, polymorphism, and inheritance. OOP is defined as follows: It is a method of programming in which programs are organized as co-operative collections of objects, each of which represents an instance of some class and whose classes are all members of a hierarchy of classes united through the property called inheritance.

CHAPTER EIGHT

Planning a Computer Program

Planning a computer program is nothing but planning the logic of the program. In order to produce a correct and effective computer program, the logic of the program has to be planned first. Without having the logic, a programmer can't write the program well.

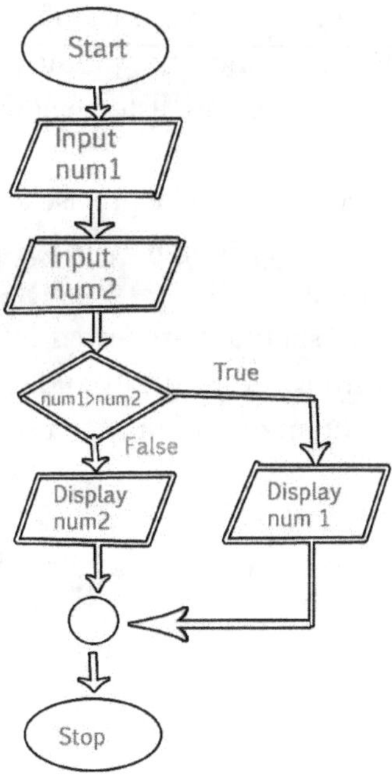

Fig. 8.1 Planning a Program using Flowchart

In a computer program, all the instructions must be written in a proper sequence. When the order is not correct or some of the instructions are left out, the computer will calculate a wrong answer. To ensure the correct order and the appropriateness of the computer instructions, a program must be planned first. Planning a computer program is done with the help of planning tools and techniques, which include Algorithm, Flowchart and Pseudo code.

A sequence of instructions is called an algorithm. Writing algorithm is a fundamental part of computing. Flowcharts and Pseudo code are the two commonly used tools for designing the program logic (also called algorithm). Generally, flowcharts work well for small problems but Pseudo code is used for larger problems.

Using Algorithm

The term algorithm refers to the logic of the program. An algorithm is defined as a step-by-step description of how to arrive at the solution of a given problem. Algorithm contains a set of instructions that must be executed in a specified sequence to produce a desired result. The characteristics of a good algorithm are listed below:

1. Each and every instruction should be precise and unambiguous.
2. Each instruction should be designed in such a way that it can be performed in a finite time.
3. Not a single instruction should be repeated infinitely, i.e., there should be an end for an algorithm both logically and physically.
4. After the termination of an execution, the user must be able to get the desired output.

The following are three ways in which an algorithm can be represented:

- As Programs
- As Flowcharts
- As Pseudo codes

The first one is the language representation of an algorithm that can be compiled and executed by a computer to produce an expected output. When a high-level language is used for representing an algorithm, it becomes a computer program. The syntax and semantics of that particular programming language must be followed to write the program in it.

Normally an algorithm is written in simple and plain English. No rules and regulations are formed for writing an algorithm except some characteristics, which qualify a set of instructions to be an algorithm. To represent an algorithm pictorially a flowchart is used.

Drawing Flowcharts

A flowchart is a pictorial representation of an algorithm. Programmers often use it as a visual tool for organizing the sequence of steps necessary to solve a problem. The process of drawing a flowchart for an algorithm is often referred to as flowcharting. Some of the common symbols used in flowcharts are shown below.

	Symbols	Functions
1.		Start/stop
2.		Input/output
3. 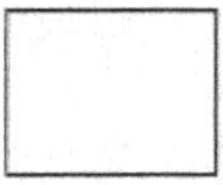		Processing
4. 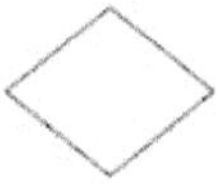		Decision Box
5. 		Flow of control
6. 		Connector

Fig. 8.2 Basic Flowchart Symbols

A set of symbols is provided for drawing a flowchart and to represent different operations to be executed by a computer. The symbols used in a flowchart are connected together using arrow headed solid lines to indicate the sequence in which the instructions must be evaluated. Flowcharting is a task that must be done after writing the algorithm for a computer program. It is a pictorial representation of a program.

With flowcharting, essential steps of an algorithm are shown using the shapes called flowchart symbols. The flow of data between steps is indicated by arrows, or flow lines.

Average of 3 Numbers - sequence

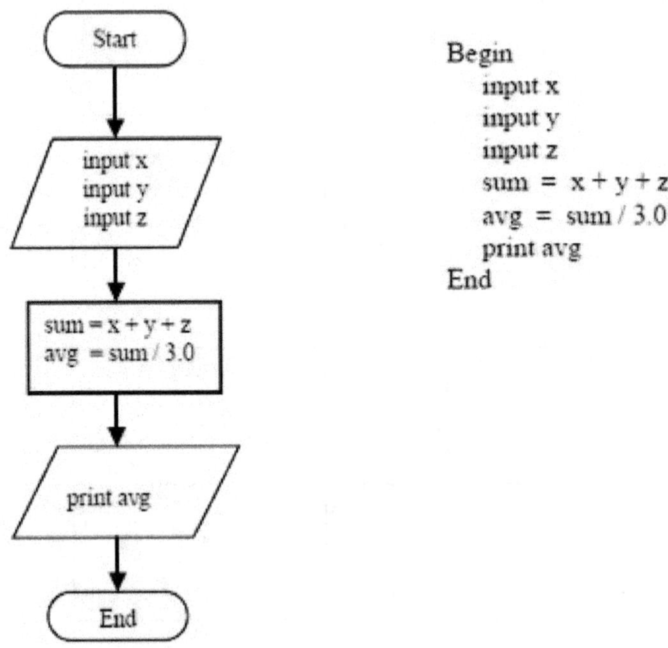

Fig. 8.3 Flowchart & Its Corresponding Pseudo Code

The flowchart shown above is for getting three values as input, and to compute the sum and average of those numbers given as input. The average value has to be displayed as output to the user.

CHAPTER NINE

Planning a Computer Program (Contd.)

The Pseudo code describes the essential steps to be taken in a program just like a flowchart, but without the graphical enhancements.

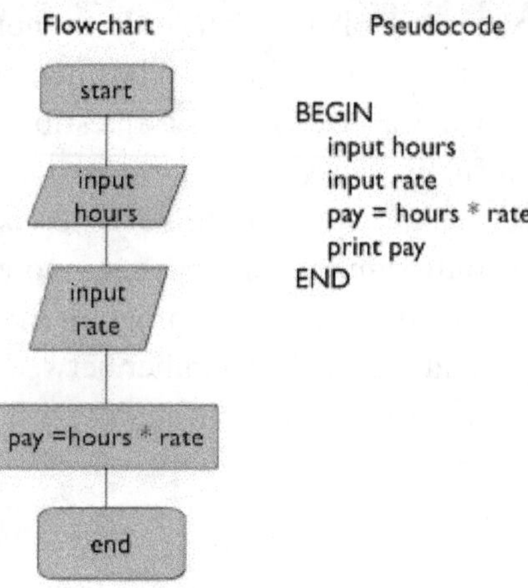

Fig. 9.1 Two Different Representations of a Program

Decision Making (Switching logic)

Switching logic consists of two components - a condition and a goto command that gets executed depending on the result of the condition test. The condition is formed using one of the six mathematical relations symbolized below:

    == Equals

!= Not Equal

< Less than

<= Less than or equal to

> Greater than

>= Greater than or equal to

In practice, the computer is presented not with a true/false statement, but with a question that results either in "Yes" or "No" answer. For example if A = 10, B = 20, K = 5, and SALES = 10000, then the conditions and their results are as follows:

Is A == B? No

Is B > A? Yes

Is K <= 25? Yes

Is SALES >= $5000.00? Yes

While evaluating each condition (question) given above, the computer will take a different course of action depending on the answer it obtains.

In general, a step in an algorithm that leads to more than one possible continuation is called a decision. In flowcharting, the diamond-shaped symbol is used to indicate a decision. The question is placed inside the symbol, and each alternative answer to the question is used to label the exit arrow which leads to the appropriate next step of the algorithm. The decision symbol is the only symbol that may have more than one exit.

The below example is a flowchart for a program that reads two numbers and displays the bigger and the smaller number between those two numbers :

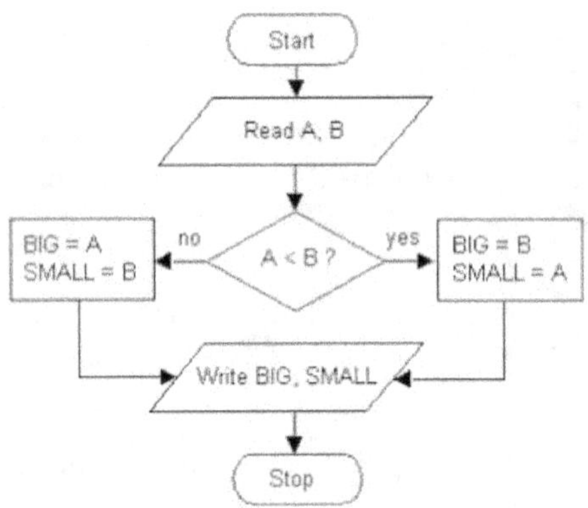

Fig. 9.2 Flowchart for Finding the Greatest of Two Numbers

The equivalent Pseudo code of the above flowchart is shown below. Note that while writing the Pseudo code, indentation is used to show the steps to follow when a condition (decision) is true:

Read A, B
If A is less than B
BIG = B
SMALL = A
else
BIG = A
SMALL = B
Write (Display) BIG, SMALL

Looping Process

Most programs involve repeating a series of instructions over and over until some event occurs. This repetitive operation is also known as looping or iterative process. Iteration is a repetitive process in which the program must count the number of times a certain operation occurs. For example, if we wish to read ten numbers and compute the average, we need a loop to count the number of times we have read the input.

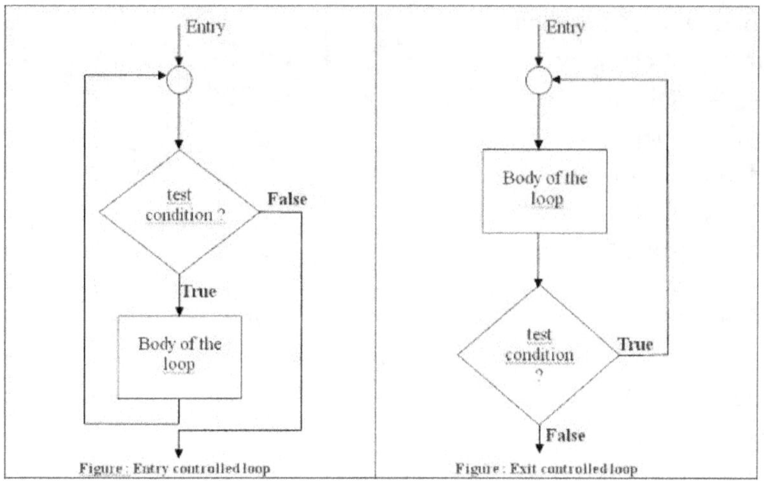

Fig. 9.3 Types of Looping - Entry Controlled and Exit Controlled

Among the flowcharts shown above, the one at the left represents an entry controlled loop, where as the flowchart at the right represent an exit-controlled loop. Entry controlled loop check the condition first and then executes the loop, if the condition evaluates to true. On the other hand, exit controlled loop executes the body of the loop at least once whether the condition is true or false. Only at the end of the first iteration, the condition is evaluated.

In many cases we do not know how many times we want to do something. The number of iterations often dependent on the data provided to the program at runtime. In that case, we can go for while loop which iterates 'n' times based on value of a variable.

Here is a problem that needs iteration: Read n numbers from the user and compute the average of all the given numbers. In this problem, we don't know how many numbers are to be read, but will read numbers until there are no more. Two alternative solutions are there for this kind of problem:

Pre-test loop:

```
set average to zero
    set count to zero
    set total to zero
    read number
    while ( not end-of-data )
    increment count by 1
    total = total + number
    read number
    if ( count > 0 ) then
    average = total / count
    display average
```

Post-test loop:

```
set count to zero
    set total to zero
    set average to zero
    do
    read a number
    increment count by 1
```

total = total + number
while (not end-of-data)
if (count > 0) then
average = total / count
display average

The above two versions of pseudo code assume that the computer will inform the program when there are no more numbers in the input. This is called an end-of-data or end-of-file test.

There is an important difference between the pre-test and post-test loops. The pre-test version will not execute its body if there is no input given by the user, whereas the post-test version executes the body of the loop at least once.

Basics of C Programming

This section introduces the basic concepts of C Programming, which include the following:

CHAPTER TEN

Introduction to C Programming

'C' is a structured, high-level, machine independent language. The early version of 'C' developed during 1970s is known as 'Traditional C'. Then, in the year 1989, 'ANSI C' was written to meet the standards set by the American National Standards Institute (ANSI) to become a standard structured programming language.

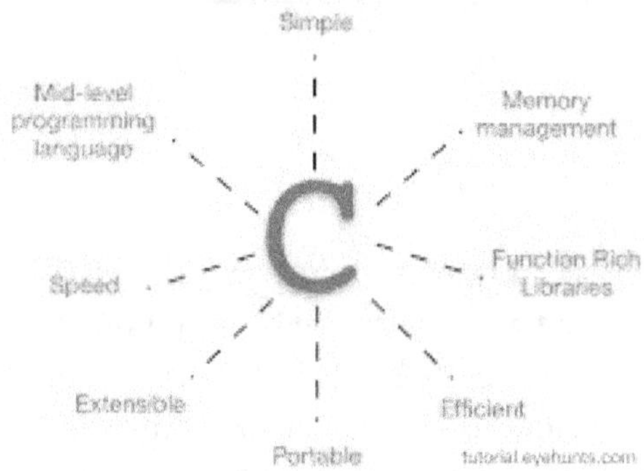

Fig. 10.1 Some of the Features of C Language

In the early 1960s, the language ALGOL was introduced. It was the first structured programming language. In 1967, Martin Richards developed a language called BCPL (Basic Combined Programming Language) primarily for writing system software. In 1970, Ken Thompson created another language called 'B' based on many features of BCPL.

The language 'B' was used for creating the early versions of UNIX OS. Finally, the language 'C' was developed based on many concepts of its predecessors by Dennis Ritchie at Bell Laboratories in 1972. The later versions of UNIX were coded almost entirely in C.

Characteristics of C:

'C' language became very popular because of its special features as listed below:

1. It provides a rich set of built-in-functions and operators using which complex programs can be easily written.
2. It combines the capabilities of an assembly language with the features of a high-level language. Therefore it is well suited for writing both system software and application packages.
3. It has a variety of data types for efficient storage and operation.
4. It is highly portable. That means the programs written in C for one computer can run on another with little or no modification.
5. It promotes modularity in writing software by allowing the programs to be written as modules or sub programs. The name given for a sub program is 'Function'.

Structure of 'C' Program

The general basic structure of a C program is shown in the figure below. Program execution begins with the body of the function main(), which is enclosed within curly braces: "{" and "}". Function main() may contain both local variable declarations as well as one or more executable statements.

The function main() can be preceded by other sections that include documentation, preprocessor statements and global declarations.

Documentation Section:

The documentation section consists of a set of comment lines that can contain the name of the program, the author name and other information, which the programmer would like to use later.

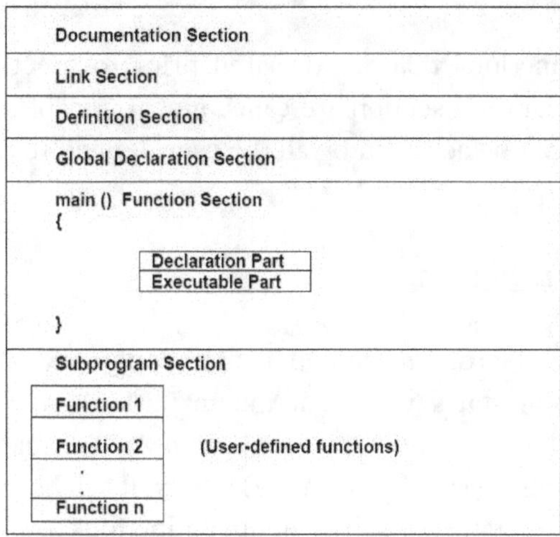

Fig. 10.2 Basic Structure of a C Porgoram

Preprocessor Statements:

The preprocessor statements begin with # symbol and are also called the preprocessor directive. These statements instruct the compiler to perform certain operations such as including header files or assigning values to constants (called symbolic constants) before starting the compilation process. Some of the preprocessor statements are listed below.

Fig. 10.2 Preprocessor Directives in C

Global Declaration Section:

The variables/functions that are declared prior to function main(), i.e., in the global declaration section are called global variables/functions. The global variables can be accessed by all the user defined functions including function main().

The main ( ) function:

Each and Every C program should contain only one main() function. Program execution starts with function main(). No C program can be written and executed without function main(). The main() function is generally written using small (lowercase) letters. It can be written using one or more executable statements, user defined functions or library functions.

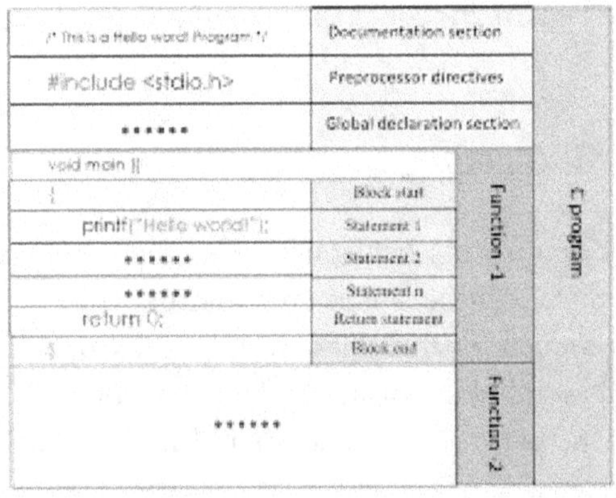

Fig. 10.3 Illustration of Various Sections of a C Program

Braces:

The statements within function main() should be enclosed with in a pair of curly braces ({, }). The left brace indicates the beginning and the right brace indicates the end of the function main(). Here are some other usages of curly braces:

1. To indicate the beginning and end of user-defined functions.

2. To enclose compound statements in a program.

Local Declarations:

The variable declaration is the first part of every C function that includes function main(). Variables declared within a function are called local variables. Here is an example of declaring local variables in function main():

1. main() {
2. int sum = 0;
3. int x;
4. float y;
5. }

In this example, the variables sum and x are declared as variables of type integer. Hence, they can be used for storing only integers throughout the program. Moreover the variable sum is initialized to zero at the time of declaration, i.e., its initial value is 0. There is one more variable named y that has been declared as a variable of type float for holding a floating point value within function main().

Program statements:

Statements are the sequence of instructions given in a program for performing certain operation using computer. They give instruction to the computer to perform a specific task (operation). An instruction is given using anyone of the following statements:

1. Input / Output statement
2. Assignment statement
3. Conditional Control statement
4. Comments that are enclosed within /* and */

The comments are not compiled and executed by the compiler. Except comments all other statements are compiled and executed by the computer at run time. They must all end with a semicolon.

User defined functions:

User defined functions are subprograms written for performing a specific operation within a C program. Each subprogram contains a set of statements for performing a specific task. They are defined outside the function main(), and are placed either before or after the main() function.

Here is a simple C program with function main() that will display a welcome message to the user:

1. #include <stdio.h>
2. main()
3. {
4. printf("Welcome to the world of C\n");
5. }

Sample C Program:

Here is a C Program for multiplying two numbers:

1. #include <stdio.h>
2. int main(){
3. int num1, num2, mul; // Declare variables 'num1', 'num2', 'sum', 'mul'
4. num1 = 2; // Assign 2 to variable 'num1'
5. num2 = 5; // Assign 5 to variable 'num2'
6. mul = num1 * num2; // Using '*' operator to multiple 'num1' and 'num2'
7. printf("%d", mul); // Displays 'mul' on screen
8. return 0;
9. }